MISSION TO BE HAPPY

Michael McLean

DESERET
BOOK

SALT LAKE CITY, UTAH

Library of Congress Cataloging-in-Publication Data
McLean, Michael, 1952–
    Mission to be happy / Michael McLean.
        p.   cm.
    ISBN 978-1-60641-203-9 (hardbound : alk. paper)
    1. Happiness.   2. Happiness—Religious aspects—Church of Jesus Christ of Latter-day Saints
3. Christian life—Mormon authors.   I. Title.
    BX8656.M42 2009
    242'.4—dc22   2009030077

Printed in the United States of America
Publishers Printing, Salt Lake City, Utah

10   9   8   7   6   5   4   3   2   1

CONTENTS

INTRODUCTION

My first thought when I felt "the call" to go on a full-time Mission 2B☺ was this: Where's the handbook? Not just any handbook, but an Official Handbook that could accommodate even a middle-aged, clinically depressed, type 2 diabetic. I was convinced when the call came that I couldn't be the first person in the world to be making a mission out of finding greater happiness. But since I couldn't find a handbook, I decided to put one together myself—something to guide me through my quest to be genuinely, authentically, and verifiably happy. And I'm not talking about any phony baloney, fake-grinning, pretend sort of happy. I'm not talking about a once-in-a-while or a just-won-a-car-on-*The-Price-Is-Right* kind of happy. I'm talking about the real deal.

So an Official Handbook was critical for a guy like me who's missed more than a few brilliantly happy moments because I was distracted by . . . what do you call it? . . . that thing . . . you know that thing where you get up every day and have to figure out how to pay the rent and keep your job when the economy is falling apart? It's got a name. It's what happens when you realize you may *never* get to retire because your 401-K is now a 101-K . . . and your blood sugar is way too high even though you had the no-sugar-added ice cream (which everyone knows is icky) . . . you know what I'm talking about . . . it's that thing that gets all complicated with other people and family and relationships, which is much harder than anyone ever told you it would be, and it's *always* happening . . . that thing . . . oh, yeah . . . it's called LIFE. That thing that all too often can distract us from the most wonderful part of itself simply because we're so focused on taking all the right steps to "get to" happiness that we end up stepping *over* instead of *into* the sweetest part of being alive.

So, I've done my research and have given this handbook a collection of songs to accompany the various chapters. I've done this because, for me, songs can be the best teachers. I've never memorized a whole chapter of anything I've ever read, but I *have* found myself singing songs over and over again until their messages eventually become a part of me. So the method in my Mission 2B☺ madness is that I'm more likely to relate and respond to something that becomes a part of me than to something I'm straining to remember.

CHAPTER 1

The Mission Statement

The Official Mission Statement for a Mission 2B☺ takes the form of an anthem. And since an anthem with words but without the music cannot fill the full measure of its creation, you might want to plug in the music for full effect and get this mission off on the right foot.

No, really. Turn on the music.

Mission 2B☺

I've been called to teach the six-year-olds.
I've been called to bake the casseroles.
I've been called to help out with the Cub Scout den, again.
But I've felt a calling in my heart,
And I believe it's time I start—
So I set myself apart and had my own farewell.

On a mission to be happy,
A mission to rejoice,
On a mission where the boundaries
And rules are all my choice.
There'll be lots of opposition
But I'll give it my all
'Cause I believe that being happy's gonna
Be my favorite call.

I know I've got a lot to learn.
I feel like a fresh intern
Where the plan of happiness is my employ, oh boy!
And training comes so easily
'Cause everywhere's the MTC—
Oh, I can't wait to learn the language of joy!

On a mission to be happy,
A mission and a quest
To be celebrating daily
All the ways that I've been blessed.
And this mission's dedicated to the souls that it can help,
And my main investigator is none other than myself.

THE MISSION STATEMENT

On a mission to be happy
There's just, there's just one guarantee:
On my mission to be happy
My first convert is gonna be me!

Note: If you're not smiling a little bit, or at the very least happily tapping your toe while you listen to the M2B☺ anthem, it could be a bit of a clue that this particular mission, at least this version, may not be for you. This isn't a judgment, and you're welcome to read on and check out the songs, but I'm just sayin' . . . it's a tough beginnin' if your heart ain't grinnin'.

As with many things "mission-esque," it might be helpful to take a closer look at this musical Mission Statement and evaluate what we're taking on when we truly accept the call to go on a Mission 2B☺.

First, even if you've never been called to teach the six-year-olds *or* bake casseroles *or* serve the Cub Scouts (or participate in any other organized Church-affiliated activity), you are still absolutely, positively eligible to go on this mission. What's required here is a *willingness to learn how to* REJOICE AND CELEBRATE!

Note that the operative words are "willingness to learn how to." On this particular mission you are *not* called to learn how to be happy and then go out and share your discovery with everyone else. In other words, there's no burden to make everyone around you happy, or even to agree that the trail you're blazing to personal happiness is the one they should walk. No, no, no. Your mission, your quest, is to learn how to better celebrate daily the ways *you* have been blessed. And we're talking about blessings you may have missed out on because you were either looking for happiness in all the wrong places or not paying attention at all.

Our anthem states that the rules and the boundaries of this mission are all your choice. That doesn't mean that there aren't any rules or boundaries. There are clearly rules and boundaries, but it's only when you have chosen or discovered them and defined them as your own that they become an asset instead of an impediment.

Here's a little two-part exercise that may be helpful in illustrating the point.

Part 1: Close your eyes and count slowly and silently from one to ten.

Any problems? You don't have to do this in a foreign language. Your native tongue is fine. Just get from one to ten and open your eyes.

Great. Now the second part of this little exercise.

Wait. Before we go to part two, I need to know if you're familiar with *chocolate*. Doesn't matter which kind of chocolate: Swiss chocolate, dark chocolate, hot chocolate, chocolate ice cream, chocolate cake, chocolate candies, chocolate malted milkshakes. Anything that qualifies as that delicious brown sweet substance that actually forms one of the major food groups in some people's diets. If for dietary reasons you're unfamiliar with any and all things chocolate, you're excused from this little test. Okay. We can move on.

Part 2: Close your eyes and count slowly and silently from one to ten without thinking about chocolate! If anything chocolate enters your mind at any time during your counting, you have to stop and start over again, beginning at one.

You might want to think about something that's *not* chocolate to keep your mind off chocolate, but this can be a tricky strategy. Thinking about that other thing might simply remind you that you're only focusing on it because you're not supposed to be thinking about the chocolate that this other thing is meant to distract you from thinking about. Just don't think about chocolate. Stop it! If you can't stop it before you start, you're never going to make it from one to ten without thinking about anything that melts in your mouth, not in your hands. . . . Ignore that. If you have a marker, go ahead and scratch those lines out. Just don't use a *brown* one.

Okay, begin.

Why is this taking you soooooo long? You did this counting effortlessly in Part 1. What happened?

The Official M2B☺ Handbook would like to suggest what might have happened. In each case the goal was the same: to count from one to ten. But when the focus was not on the goal but on what we *weren't supposed to do* while trying to reach that goal, everything became more difficult than it needed to be.

Life can do that to us. Distract us. Become the urgent, demanding, have-to-deal-with-right-now sequence of things that keeps us from celebrating and rejoicing in the little miracles of happiness that are begging for our attention. Remember, our mission is to be "willing to learn" how to celebrate and rejoice in the ways we've been blessed, to find happiness where we haven't found it before.

Another thing that probably should be highlighted here before we move on is that bit about learning a new language: the language of *joy*.

Those of us who are not natural linguists may be concerned about the foreign language required for this mission. Some of us aren't familiar with the language of joy at all. Others may think they know what it sounds like, but they might be wrong.

The language of joy is not at all the same as what some might call "happy-speak." Happy-speak is really a pseudo-language, like pig Latin. It's a made-up way of communicating in which people can pretend that the real tragedies and heartaches of the world will be minimized if they just say the correct happy-speak words to make everything okay. On a mission to be happy, the real happiness we seek is not found in glossing over and denying the truths of life, plugging our fingers in our ears as we loudly sing, "La-la-la-la-la, I'm not listening!" No, the language of joy is nothing if not honest, tender, and kind. The language of joy is spoken in truth every single moment, with a faith that prevails even when we don't really understand why something impossibly difficult has happened to us or to someone we love. Pretending we understand when we don't is a poor substitute for trusting the Source of happiness to reveal the answers when we're truly ready to receive them.

The reason it's ultimately important to learn the language of joy is not so much for the benefit of others, but for ourselves. If we can learn to think in this language, there's an excellent chance that we'll be able to place in our hearts and minds language-of-joy descriptions of the "real deal" when it comes to happiness.

CHAPTER 2

Knowing When You're Ready

I don't suspect anyone would respond to the call to go on a Mission 2B☺ if something deep inside didn't confirm that this was something they needed to do. My own reasons for accepting the call may not be the same as yours. You may have experienced any number of things that have kept you from finding the happiness you believe should accompany your journey here on earth. Typically no one gets called on a M2B☺ until they discover they're sick and tired of being sick and tired.

Now would be the time you play the music. Although there won't be a quiz, the song will get you in the spirit of this chapter.

Sick 'n Tired

Guess I was wishful. I took a fistful
Of every vitamin that's known to man.
I read their letter. Said I'd feel better

After a couple months on their plan.
Before and after pictures tell the tale;
I still look overweight and somewhat pale—well I'm

Sick 'n tired of being sick 'n tired,
Tired of justifying my malaise,
Sick 'n tired of feeling uninspired,
But I've acquired a new fire these days:
I'm sick and tired enough to change my ways.

So here's a shocker. I asked my doctor
If his prescriptions came with guarantees.
All that was certain, besides my hurtin',
Is what he'd charge me for his doctor fees.
'Cause all the medicine that he prescribed
Could only work with what I felt inside, and I'm

Sick 'n tired of being sick 'n tired,
Tired of justifying my malaise,
Sick 'n tired of feeling uninspired,
But I've acquired a new fire these days:
I'm sick and tired enough to change my ways.

So what's the answer? I don't have cancer,
But I've been feelin' lousy for a while.
I think I see, yeah, I've had amnesia,
I have forgotten all my reasons to smile.
I think it's time I put my hand to the plough;
I'm sick 'n tired enough to make some changes now, 'cause I'm

Sick 'n tired of being sick 'n tired,
Tired of justifying my malaise,
Sick 'n tired of feeling uninspired,
But I've acquired a new fire these days:
I'm sick and tired enough to change my ways.

It's important to stress, right here in the early chapters of the Official Handbook, that the goal of this mission is *not* to try to alter the fundamental nature of life. Life often teaches us its most profound lessons by challenging us and testing us and giving us opportunities to grow . . . you know, all that hard stuff. Our goal, rather, is to fundamentally alter the way we experience our lives. And that's why our mission is not measured in years or months or weeks or days but in *moments*.

Yikes! You mean once I'm committed to being on a Mission 2B☺ it's *forever?*

And once I've felt the call and had my own farewell, there's no homecoming to look forward to when my mission is over? No report of the marvelous things I've learned?

That's right. As you may have noticed from the Mission 2B☺ anthem, from the second you begin your mission, everywhere you are is where your mission is. You can't come home from it because you never leave. Furthermore, your happiness isn't something that will happen when (or after) you've followed a carefully laid-out, step-by-step program to be happy. Mission 2B☺ missionaries do not think in terms of "I'll be happy when *this* happens or when *that* has been accomplished." The happiness has to be in the present moment or we're going to miss it.

A Mission 2B☺ is a *now* experience, not a *when* experience. And *now* is as good a time as any to examine your life and decide if you're sick 'n tired of bein' sick 'n tired. If you are, the happy news is you can choose to change. The exciting thing about being on a Mission 2B☺ is that you'll acquire a new fire—if you're sick 'n tired enough to change your ways.

CHAPTER 3

THE PHYSICAL

Don't get the wrong idea. Anyone can go on a Mission 2B☺ regardless of his or her physical condition. But there are conditions like clinical depression that may prevent a person from being able to make the sort of choices that will have to be made in order to have a successful mission. If that's the case for you, it's important to get help! You can get it while you're on your mission, or as an integral part of your mission, but getting healthy and balanced is part of the deal you're making with yourself.

Now, professional therapists, psychologists, psychiatrists, and counselors are not all inspired "genius-angels" who will heal you of your mental and/or emotional illnesses. But compared to people with profoundly deep psychological wounds or chemical imbalances in their brains who are trying to sort things out on their own, they're pretty close. I know there are those whose life journey has brought them to different conclusions than mine, and I respect their experience and believe it's every bit as valid and probably worth even more serious consideration than mine. But since I'm writing the handbook, I have only my personal experience to share on this one. Were it not for the gift of therapists, medical doctors, scientists, (dare I say it) drug manufacturers, and those patient and loving friends and family members who helped me find the right combination of all these genius-angels, I could never have even considered the idea of a Mission 2B☺.

In addition to the stuff that's broken in my brain, I have a broken pancreas, along with various and sundry signs of decrepitude that accompany type 2 diabetics in the "seniors" category. So besides pills and shots and dietary restrictions, I have a non-negotiable requirement for regular exercise. These are current "givens" if I'm to be functional on this mission. I'm choosing to be grateful for the help.

But getting the song right for this chapter has been a real challenge for me. With each attempt, I struggled to capture what this middle-aged, clinically depressed, type 2 diabetic needed to hear. Too many of the songs I tried to write sounded way too much like every other song I've written to help me get through dark and difficult times. But the one that found its way into this collection turned out to be a surprisingly upbeat, toe-tapping, self-deprecating yet fun exploration of something that I take very seriously: my dependence on heavenly help to get through each and every moment of each and every day.

I'm dependent on pills, and on insulin and doctors and a daily regimen, but mostly I'm dependent on a Higher Power, a kind, wise Heavenly Friend who I believe wants every Mission 2B☺ to be a success. The song, it turns out, is my rebuttal to the years and years I spent praying for the Lord to heal me and being upset that He wouldn't do it the way I wanted, when I wanted. The song reminds me that my preconceived notions about how the Lord operates when it comes to healing His children lacked the kind of faith that got me to the clinic, the therapist, and the pharmacy, where I could discover all that God had already done to help me. I guess on a Mission 2B☺ it's a good idea to be humble enough to see life from a point of view far less limited than your own.

For those of you who may suffer from some of my same afflictions, I'm confessing that I got discouraged when I realized that it had taken me sooooo long to figure this stuff out. And, as we all know, there's nothing in Satan's arsenal quite as effective as discouragement to keep us from finding the happiness that can enrich each day. So when I find myself slipping over to the dark side, I turn this song up real loud, and when it's done, I'm smiling again at this Mission 2B☺ realization: The pills aren't healing me. He is. And I'm so grateful He helped me learn how much He loves me and has always loved me, even when I couldn't see it.

Pills

Something's broken in my brain
And only pills can fix it.
I fought this thing for years in vain,
Believing I could lick it.
I tried and failed and felt so weak,
It made me quite the cynic.

And then I heard heaven speak:
"Hey, get thee to a clinic."
I thought that meant the clinic
For my own immortal soul,
So I trudged down to a church to wait
For a miracle to make me whole.
Then something happened then and there that came as quite a shocker:
I heard a voice from up Above say, "I meant get thee to a doctor."

Hey, son, you need pills.
They can't cure all your ills.
I know you pray it'll change, but the truth is still:
Sonny, you need pills.

I said, "But You're the Power of heaven and earth,
Creator, King, and Master—
So, why not just heal me here and now?
It's cheaper and it's faster."
He paused so long I thought He'd gone,
Then added this to my story:
"There's no shame in a broken brain,
So don't be self-incriminatory."

14

Hey, son, you need pills.
No, they can't cure all your ills.
I know you pray it'll change, and it probably will
If you'll just take your pills.

He told me, "Guess who guided scientists to understand exactly what's wrong
With you and make up some medicines so you can carry on?
You see, I know you wonder if I hear
Your prayers when you say them.
Well, I've truly heard your cries for help
Long before you pray them."

Trust me, you need pills,
Although they can't cure all your ills.
I know you pray it'll change, but my advice is still:
Sonny, take your pills.

Hey, son, take your pills.
No, they can't cure all your ills.
I know you pray it'll change, but the truth is still—
So take some advice,
Don't you think twice—
You really need pills.

CHAPTER 4

Adjusting for Circumstance

Sometimes circumstances in our lives keep trying to distract us from being happy and at peace in the moment. Sometimes it feels hypocritical to even *think* we could find happiness when there is so much sorrow surrounding us. If that's true for you right now, please believe me when I tell you that you *can* find the faith that says: I don't understand, and I don't know how long this is going to last—this situation may seem permanent, but how I experience this moment is not permanent, as long as my language of joy tells me the truth about what's going on. I can still be happy: IF I don't color that truth with anger or frustration that I can't change what's going on; and IF I don't refuse to accept it because it's not how I wanted or planned or hoped it would be; and IF I don't blame the situation on someone or something else and believe that my inner hero could swoop in and save the day if only the idiots who made this mess would let me.

What if, instead, I choose to see the circumstance for what it truly is and ask:

Who am I going to trust to know best how to find the good in this situation? Am I picking me, with all my profound wisdom, insight, and backlog of inspired truths archived in my spectacularly brilliant brain? Or do I trust a Higher Intelligence, a Truer Source, a Greater Power? Let's review. I can trust me or I can trust God. Ummmm—is this a trick question?

Yes, it is! Most all people in the world *say* they trust God, but they really only trust themselves. Absolutely trusting God requires us to stop pretending we know His will in this moment because we have read about (and think we understand) how He manifested His will in some other moment! The Bible has a number of really great examples of this phenomenon, but for this handbook I would like to draw our attention to one in particular.

There's a fascinating moment in the New Testament where a fellow comes to Jesus and asks what else he must do to be a true follower. Jesus gets a sense of the man and in that moment suggests he sell everything he owns and give it to the poor. Wow, the guy didn't see *that* coming; he apparently has lots and lots of really cool stuff. So he takes his name off the disciple list and leaves. The Apostles see this and make mental notes: *Followers of Jesus are willing to sell their stuff and help out the poor. Got it.*

So, sometime later, when a woman is trying to get through the apostolic entourage and present Jesus with a sensational oil that has a reputation of making your sandal-wearing feet feel as if they already were in the kingdom of heaven, the Apostles offer her this heads-up: "Don't waste your time. Jesus isn't into expensive oils. He'd rather you sell the stuff and give it to the poor. Sorry. What did you pay for that, if you don't mind us asking?"

Before the woman can answer the Apostles, Jesus turns this moment on its head. Essentially what He says to this woman is, "Wow! Are you kidding me? You not only found what has to be the most exquisite lotion of the Middle East but you lugged it all the way up here and now you're offering my weary feet the bliss only your thoughtfulness and that oil could provide. How much do I love you!" I'd give anything to have seen the smile on that woman's face as she found her way to the open arms of Jesus of Nazareth.

Different moment, different Jesus? Or . . . was it the *same* Jesus who just knew how to follow the guidance He was given in each and every unique and precious moment?

The point of the Mission 2B☺ is to be willing to learn how to see and experience each moment as He did. So if you think for one moment that you, on your own, without one ounce of divine help, actually "get it," give it up. You really don't. That's why—and I know this from experience—we end up hating certain moments that we think are permanent, but the truth is:

You Don't Know (How Long This Thing Is Gonna Last)

You might have had a bad break
That rocked your world like an earthquake;

ADJUSTING FOR CIRCUMSTANCE

You might even believe it's the end.
The reasons for your sorrow
That poisons each tomorrow
May be much worse than mine, my friend.
But I've learned a lesson that I want to pass along.

You don't know how long this thing is gonna last.
You don't know how long until this too shall pass.
You don't know how heaven's gonna turn this around.
You don't know how wonderful it's gonna be
With a miracle you can't yet see—
Don't you disagree with me, 'cause
You don't know.

You say you don't want to hear it;
You know the truth is you fear it
Might threaten your excuse for that frown.
Well, we've all got Ph.D.s in reasons to be down.

You don't know how long this thing is gonna last.
You don't know how long until this too shall pass.
You don't know how heaven's gonna turn this around.
You don't know whose love is gonna intervene

With a gift completely unforeseen
Beyond your wildest dreams, 'cause
You don't know
What is in store for you,
Or who's been on your side to see you through?

You don't know what's goin' on that you can't see.
You don't know the lessons of your misery.
You don't know, but someday I know you will.

You don't know how long this thing is gonna last.
You don't know how long until this too shall pass.
You don't know how heaven's gonna turn this around.
You don't know how long you're gonna feel this way.
Though it seems forever, you can't say:
It all might change today—
You don't know
You don't know
You don't know

CHAPTER 5

EXPECTING THE UNEXPECTED JOY

Although we can stumble upon something we've lost by accident (like when we're cleaning or searching for something else), generally we track down the things we're looking for when we're actually *looking* for them. "Where did I put that?" Or, "Honey, where did *you* put that?"

Well, when we're looking for happiness there is a parallel . . . sort of. For the sake of our mission, we're going to refer to two kinds of happiness: the kind we have known but somehow lost, and the brand-new happiness we discover that tickles us to death and creates a magic moment in our day.

Let's start with the "lost" happiness.

Here's a tip. Trying to re-create a remembered happiness might be a good way to remind yourself how lucky you were to have found love and joy and happiness once upon a time, but it carries with it a very real danger: *Expectations!* Remembering how great something once was, and demanding it be that way again in order to be classified as "real happiness," may be cheating a potentially sweet and wonderful new moment. Imagine: You and your beloved decide to put a happy spark of love back in your relationship, so you come up with a plan. The discussion goes something like this:

"Remember when we were first dating, and we had that amazing dinner at (fill in the blank), and you were wearing (fill in the blank) that was way beyond gorgeous and you took my breath away? And I looked, well, the way I looked twenty pounds ago and with my real hair, but you can imagine, can't you? And then that waiter with the lisp asked what we wanted for dessert and at the same moment we both said (fill in the blank), and then we looked deeply into each other's eyes because a cosmic sign had just been given that we were meant for each other. And then later, when we kissed good night, there were serious, screaming 'yippee!' voices in our heads and a tingling that remained for three days. Well, I called and made a reservation at that restaurant and thought we'd go there on Friday and do *that* again. But don't feel any pressure to find that dress or wear your hair long like you did that night. I know you had to cut it short since the kids came along and totally ruined the great date part of our becoming a couple."

All right, all right. Reclaiming some happy memories doesn't have to go like that. You certainly can go back to that place, either physically or in your mind, but the joy of making a new memory there might be totally wrecked by a predetermined expectation of what is supposed to happen and how it's supposed to feel. This doesn't mean you can't find happiness in planned moments like this, but if you're not careful you'll miss the new moments by desperately longing for the old ones.

BUT! On a Mission 2B☺, *every* moment can be a chance to expect an unexpected joy. This is the second kind of happiness, the brand-new kind that you didn't even know was coming. Now, this joy doesn't have to be some hugely big deal, like your son at college calling home and not asking for money. It can be just a little something, like the "oooooh" moment I experienced before writing this chapter.

Here's the history: I was in my office doing this thing called *feng shui,* which I think is Polish for "clear out all the junk you don't need anymore and get organized." And while I was agonizing over the fate of my old record player and treasured forty-fives, I decided to put on my favorite early Beatles record: "She Loves You (Yeah, Yeah, Yeah)," and I was suddenly drifting back to the days when I thought vinyl coming out of a crackly three-inch speaker sounded cool. Then, unexpectedly, at exactly one minute and two seconds into the song, I spontaneously found myself joining Paul and John singing *Oooooh!* It was an amazing moment. Then it happened again at precisely one minute and forty seconds into the song: *Oooooh!* Wow! What a feeling! The *oooooh* itself didn't last that long, but the spontaneous joy of singing it lingered longer than I ever could have imagined.

So, in celebration of that moment, and to remind me on my Mission 2B☺ that this is but one tiny little example of what awaits us if we're open to it, I offer this song.

With Paul and John

I wonder if I am
The only one who knows about this?
Should I call my lawyer and
Get a patent on my newfound bliss?
My favorite four-piece band,
At sixty-two seconds in,
Made my heart have to grin.

It happened once again
At a hundred seconds on the nose.
I do that thing and then
The smile inside me grows.
I'm tellin' you, my friend,
You ought to try it yourself.
I promise it really helps.

Every time I sing "oooooh"
With Paul and John,
While I'm singing "oooooh"
It feels like nothin' can go wrong;
All my fears and worries are gone

EXPECTING THE UNEXPECTED JOY

When I sing "oooooh"
With Paul and John.

This may not be your style,
'Cause the Beatles may not be your band.
It might not bring a smile
Like mine, you know I understand.
But join me for a while—
It's just a couple of "ooooohs"
That might erase all your blues.

Every time I sing "oooooh"
With John and Paul,
While I'm singing "ooooooh"
It seems I got no problems at all.
The insurmountable seems small
When I sing "oooooh"
With John and Paul.

So when the song is through
And you've got to face the world once again,
Just remember something you
Can do to brighten up a dreary regimen.

When you sing the magic "oooooh,"
Shake your head a little longer—
It makes the feeling stronger.

Every time I sing "oooooh"
With John and Paul,
While I'm singing "oooooh"
It seems I got no problems at all.
The insurmountable seems small
When I sing "oooooh"
With John and Paul.

Every time I sing "oooooh"
With Paul and John,
While I'm singing "oooooh"
It feels like nothin' can go wrong.
All my fears and worries are gone
When I sing "oooooh."

CHAPTER 6

Faith

For this chapter we're going to focus on the "other" John and Paul. The New Testament version. It doesn't say anything in the Bible about John or Paul being singers or songwriters. But then again, it doesn't say they couldn't have been. I bring this up only because as I write this I'm having a Mission 2B☺ moment. I'm smiling at the thought of the ancient John or Paul introducing a brand-new tune at one of their Middle East mission conferences. I promise, I'm not being irreverent. Just thinking this helps me feel closer to them somehow.

But I digress. Where was I? Oh yes, the New Testament. I love that book, and as I read it I notice that Paul in particular has something important to tell us about faith. Since a significant amount of faith is essential in order for a Mission 2B☺ to bless our lives, let's liken what he said way back then to the moments we're experiencing way right now.

I'll focus on this: "Faith is the substance [assurance] of things hoped for, the evidence [proof] of things not seen" (Hebrews 11:1).

Here's the Mission 2B☺ thing about faith. Sacred texts tell us that asking God for "signs" can be a dangerous and hurtful thing, but *come on,* missionaries, we gotta get something, *sometime,* or we'll quit having faith. In the Gospel According to John there's a passage where a man asks Jesus to come and heal his son, who is dying.

"Then said Jesus unto him, Except ye see signs and wonders, ye will not believe.

"The nobleman saith unto him, Sir, come down ere my child die.

"Jesus saith unto him, Go thy way; thy son liveth. And the man believed the word that Jesus had spoken unto him, and he went his way.

"And as he was now going down, his servants met him, and told him, saying, Thy son liveth.

"Then enquired he of them the hour when he began to amend. And they said unto him, Yesterday at the seventh hour the fever left him.

"So the father knew that it was at the same hour, in the which Jesus said unto him, Thy son liveth: and himself believed, and his whole house" (John 4:48-53).

From my reading of the text I don't see a "wicked and adulterous" man seeking signs. I see a man needing help. He had hope and he believed, but he didn't know in advance how it was all going to turn out. I get the sense that the father with a sick child had enough faith and hope to approach Jesus with a deeply felt need.

I trust that God is way smarter at knowing how to nurture our faith than we are, so whining and moaning about needing a faith-promoting moment isn't what I'm talking about. But on this mission we are permitted (and encouraged) to point out in our prayers that we're taking stuff on faith for as long as it takes, but we're *also* humbly asking (like the father in the scripture) for the continued *gift* that faith is, whether we deserve it or not. We acknowledge that faith is a precious thing, and it can also be a fragile thing. So on a Mission 2B☺ we are encouraged to pray in the language of joy and honestly tell a loving heavenly parent that we'd appreciate a little something, sometime, somewhere giving us just enough to keep this up, so our next prayer we won't need a sign.

Remember how we talked in the last chapter about expecting the unexpected happiness? The principle holds true for faith as well. Faith-building moments can and often do come in unexpected ways, unexpected times, and unexpected places.

This song came to me unexpectedly with the ghosts of the Electric Light Orchestra playing and singing all the parts.

Push play.

I Don't Need a Sign

Faith is the substance of things hoped for
And the evidence of things not seen.
I've read it a thousand times or more,
But I'm still figuring out what it means.

I've heard the warnings
About asking for signs, well—

I don't need a sign this time,
I'm taking it on faith.
I don't need a sign this time,
But I'd appreciate
A little something, sometime, somewhere,
Givin' me just enough to keep it up so my next prayer
I won't need a sign.

Faith is the substance of things hoped for
And the evidence of things not seen.
It is a truth I can't ignore,
But I'm still figuring out what it means.

Can one be faithful
And need a witness too?

I don't need a sign this time,
I'm taking it on faith.
I don't need a sign this time

FAITH

But I'd appreciate
A little something, sometime, somewhere,
Givin' me just enough to keep it up so my next prayer
I won't need a sign.

I don't need a sign this time,
I'm taking it on faith.
I don't need a sign this time,
But I'd appreciate
A little something, sometime, somewhere,
Givin' me just enough to keep it up so my next prayer
I won't need a sign.

CHAPTER 7

Your Happiness, Your Way

This is what I'm calling the Burger King chapter. It's about having your happiness, your way.

Maybe you've been through a bad patch, and there hasn't been much happiness in your day-to-day life, but you know people who appear to be happy. It's natural to think that if you just did what they're doing, you'd turn out to be as happy as they are. Not necessarily a horrible strategy, but problematic. Sure, you can pretend to be someone else with the hope that you will find your joy the way they have found theirs. However, that joy generally won't be as sweet or as real as the joy you feel when you are absolutely, authentically you. But what does that even mean?

Great question. I don't know. I have no idea what the real, true, authentic you is like. I'm still figuring out what the real, true *me* is like. I do know there's a difference between trying to be the best, most authentic me I can be at any given moment and trying to be someone else.

Now, I have to pause and acknowledge a truth: We're *all* influenced by others. From the moment we're born, the influencing begins. We learn what we like by mimicking what others seem to like. And often we "borrow" their desires and make them our own. As a kid, I believed that if I had the exact same sneakers as Paul Rosander, I'd not only be able to run as fast as he could but I'd become as cool as he was. I would acquire a part of his identity by getting my mom to buy me the same shoes he wore to school.

On a Mission 2B☺ we get to *choose* who influences us. In fact, that may be the most important decision we make. Don't misunderstand what I'm about to say, because I know that a Mission 2B☺ is not the same mission Jesus served, but it's never a bad idea to follow His perfect example. And He *chose* Heavenly Father as the One who would influence Him most.

So, you may ask, how do we know if we've got the right idea about what Heavenly Father is *really* like?

Answer: We don't know. He does. You see, having a spiritual knowledge, given by the Holy Spirit, that He lives and loves us is not the same thing as knowing what God is like. That's the quest: "This is life eternal, that they might know thee the only true God, and Jesus Christ, whom thou hast sent" (John 17:3). Figuring out what God is really like and then choosing to be influenced by Him is the point. Further, we need to decide right at the beginning of our Mission 2B☺ that we just don't *ever* know more than He does. EVER! We're going to let Him teach us who we are and whose we are.

God's desire for us to worship Him is not because His ego is fragile and He needs our validation. He invites us to worship Him because He knows we become like what we worship, and He wants us to share in His incomprehensible joy.

The exciting news, if you can absorb it in the right light, is that the *real* you is utterly unique. Nowhere in the sacred texts will you find God asking you to betray your uniqueness. In fact, God's plan for our happiness is His celebration of our extraordinary individuality. God didn't craft puppets, He enabled intelligences to find fullness and completion. And He mentioned on more than one occasion that we would learn all this by our own experience, not someone else's.

So, as we do our push-ups or run on the treadmill to the tune of this Mission 2B☺ medley, we are committing ourselves to trust the Source of all happiness to reveal the happiness we could be missing if we trusted some other source.

Someone Else

I am seeing my reflection
Through somebody else's eyes.
I can't tell which part is me and which part is a bad disguise.
I am hearing my opinion
Through somebody else's ears.
I can barely recognize my hopes, my dreams, and all my fears.

I'm someone's neighbor,
I'm someone's child and someone's friend,

And they see through me with their own peculiar lens.
I'm carving out a place for me with someone else's knife.
Could it be that I am living someone else's life?

I am writing my life's story
With somebody else's pen.
Think I really need to find my own and start all over again.

I'm someone's neighbor,
I'm someone's child and someone's friend,
And they see through me with their own peculiar lens.
I'm carving out a place for me with someone else's knife.
Could it be that I am living someone else's life?

I am seeing my reflection
Through somebody else's eyes.
I can't tell which part is me and which part is a bad disguise.

I've Got to Find Out Who I Am

The melody's familiar;
I've heard this song before.

It's been around ten thousand years
Or maybe even more.
And everybody's sung it,
At least I think they've tried,
But even when the singing's done
This song goes on inside.

I've got to find out who I am.
I've got to find out who I am.
Got to know and got to see what's making me,
I've got to find out who I am.
I've got to find out who I am.
And when I do I know I'll be all I can,
When I find out who I am.

You're Not the Sequel

It wasn't as good as the one before,
And halfway through we got kind of bored.
We should have waited to rent the DVD.
What was missing was that great spark,
The honest moments straight from the heart—
It's what we lined up again and again to see, didn't we?

You're not the sequel.
You're not the prequel.
You're the original we love best.
Fight the temptation
For cheap imitation.
There's no consolation prize for a life second-guessed.

You can't see it but trust me, love,
Your very essence ranks high above
All of the posers just cloning every trend.
Don't be distracted by what they do,
It's not a style that looks good on you.
Genuine articles don't need to pretend, my friend.

You're not the sequel.
You're not the prequel.
You're the original we love best.
Fight the temptation
For cheap imitation.
There's no consolation prize for a life second-guessed.

And just because it's a lonely path
Doesn't mean it's the wrong one.

You're going to find in the aftermath
Your life was the sweetest song sung.

You're not the sequel.
You're not the prequel.
You're the original we love best.
Fight the temptation
For cheap imitation.
There's no consolation prize for a life second-guessed.

(Descant)
You're one of a kind,
Such a rare thing to find,
A truly original mind.
If you can't see it, you're blind.

CHAPTER 8

COMPANIONS

It's a fundamental principle that happiness increases on this mission when we celebrate not just our own uniqueness but also the diversity of those who can bless and enrich our lives. I stumbled upon this truth pre–Mission 2B☺, and I feel it's a handbook-worthy anecdote.

Over twenty years ago, a group that called themselves the Black Gospel Music Workshop of America chose Salt Lake City for their convention. Ten thousand strong, it was an amazing group of singers, conductors, composers, and musicians gathered in the shadows of the everlasting hills. Throughout their stay they presented several performances at the Salt Palace, along with a visit to the Mormon Tabernacle Choir's broadcast of *Music and the Spoken Word* featuring one of the workshop's renowned guest conductors. My black-gospel-music-singing friends were so excited to share this event with me, and one friend even invited me to participate in a performance scheduled for the Salt Palace.

"My people are coming to Salt Lake City and I want to sing one of your songs for them," she said. "Will you accompany me?"

"I'm honored," I told her, "but why do you want to sing a blue-eyed spiritual song by a wussy white guy when you've got the four-octave range that can really explode on black gospel music?"

She said, "Because *my* people need to hear me sing a song that's reflective of my newfound faith." (She and her family had recently joined the Mormon church and had heard me sing my song "You're Not Alone" at a conference I attended.)

So I asked her, "When should we get together and practice?"

"No need to practice," she answered. "Just let the Spirit be your guide."

"What key should the Spirit guide me in?" was my response.

"Don't worry, Michael. I can cut it in *any* key."

So I arrived at the Salt Palace at the appointed hour (we were scheduled to go on at 8:45 p.m.) and I took a look at the audience: about 8,400 black faces, 14 white (and one of those was mine). As I checked the lineup for the evening, I could see that things were running late . . . way late. Like two hours late. And as I listened, I understood why. The black gospel music groups got into their songs *soooo* deeply and repeated their call-and-response anthems with such passion that they just *couldn't* end them on time.

This didn't bother me, however. The music was *incredible!* In fact, the more I listened, the more intimidated I got. To make matters worse, Deborah asked me to sing the intro to the song, and then she would come in on the refrain.

Oh, great! I could see the review now: "Wussy White Guy Debuts Vocal Prowess at Black Gospel Music Showcase."

At 10:47 p.m. I put my hands on the piano and noticed they were trembling.

"In your hour of doubt, loneliness, or fear," I sang the opening line of my song and felt something was lacking, so, inspired by the previous performers and the audience's rapt attention, I added, "whoa-whoa." Didn't quite come out the way it had sounded in my head, but I forged ahead. "Listen to your heart and this is what you'll hear . . ."

I ran an arpeggio up to the chord that announced the beginning of the refrain, and I looked up to see that my friend's head was bowed.

I played the chord again.

Singer's head still bowed.

What was she waiting for? I was pretty sure it wasn't another white guy "whoa-whoa."

I hammered the chord one more time with a passion that could wake the dead. She then slowly raised her head and sang, "You're not aaaaaaaaaa-loooooooooooooooooone."

When I wrote "You're Not Alone," those four syllables had four corresponding notes. However, in this version there were more like *thirty!* And they were beautiful, and they were something only a black woman with a four-octave range and the soul of Mahalia Jackson could sing. *And then it happened. . . .*

Something took over my hands. I started to play my song with a different spirit, a different beat, different variations on the chords. The place erupted. People in the audience started waving their hands back and forth in time to the music. And Deborah took liberties with the melody that felt more inspired than the original melody itself.

At the end of the song's bridge, just before the final refrain, she sang a note that I think only dogs could hear. It was so high and exquisite I think it would have to be called *Z-sharp*.

At that precise moment I believe I became a "reverse Oreo." I was white on the outside but black deep down.

I heard my song as if for the first time. My friend had brought her unique contribution to the tune, and it changed my life for the better. She wasn't showing off her remarkable voice to draw attention to her vocal stylings. She was singing her heart, her testimony, her gratitude, her love for the One who promised He would never leave us alone. And as she sang, everyone in the hall knew that she *knew* He would never leave her alone.

How grateful I was at that moment that God had let me come to earth when Deborah was here to bring something to my life I never could have found without her gift.

I'm grateful we're all unique, and I'm prayerful that if I can be true to what I have to give, the world will be a more beautiful and harmonious place.

This truth, when absorbed deep down, can be a tremendous source of happiness. For those of us who are half of a couple, it can guide us to happier moments in our relationships. This requires a willingness for *you* to sing *you* and to let *me* sing *me*. When our life songs are sung in harmony, that's what the Mission 2B☺ calls oneness . . . in our hearts, in our lives, and in our world.

One

I have been wondering
About the true meaning
Of two people being
Together as one.

Is it just an ideal?
Or can it be real?
I'll tell you what I feel—
It's like a song sung.

So you sing you,
And I'll sing me.
When our lifesong is sung
In harmony,
That's oneness to me.

I don't think being of one heart
Means we both sing the same part,

So let's both make a fresh start
Defining what oneness can be.

You sing you,
And I'll sing me.
When our lifesong is sung
In harmony,
That's oneness to me.

You sing you,
And I'll sing me.
When our lifesong is sung
In harmony,
That's oneness to me.

CHAPTER 9

Getting Rid of the Negative

While we're enthusiastically celebrating the diversity in the world, it is crucial—no, dare I say, *absolutely essential*—to eliminate from our lives the forces that are not bringing out our best. In other words, we need to get rid of those so-called friends who are bringing us down.

I'm not talking about family members, you understand. There are people we'll always be sticking with, for better or for worse. But you know the kind of person I mean: the one who saps you of the energy you need to be putting into those more important relationships. On a Mission 2B☺ you have permission to give the "toodle-oo" to those people, the ones who are draining you of your joy and bringing out your worst. Get 'em out of your life. You don't have to be hurtful or mean to do this, but you have to be honest with yourself. Ask yourself this question: Are we bringing out the best in each other or not? If you're drained, worn out, less able to see good, find hope, rejoice . . . let 'em go.

The Toodle-oo

If you've tried to be understanding
To people so demanding
They could be arrested as emotional thieves—
By anyone's definition
They're a negative addition
If they've sucked the life from you so long that you can barely breathe.
Well, here's a little tip that you can take from me:

Give your time to those who need you;
Give your trust to the friends who are true.
But if you give your love to those who choose to just use you,
Give yourself permission to
Give them the toodle-oo.
Give them the toodle-oo.

It's not dereliction
To end your affliction
By simply doing what I'm talking about.
A little toodle-ooing and things will start improving.
This is a lesson I'm glad I figured out:
Some things just gotta go, when you're cleaning house.

Give your time to those who need you;
Give your trust to the friends who are true.
But if you give your love to those who choose to misuse you,
Give yourself permission to
Give them the toodle-oo.
Give them the toodle-oo.

It's not all their fault.
Wait, I take that back!
Maybe they're just bad for you,
And if that's a stone-cold fact,
Then say you're dumpin' everyone who's bringing out your worst,
And they are not the only one, but their name came up first.

Give your time to those who need you;
Give your trust to the friends who are true.
But if you give your love to those who choose to abuse you,
Give yourself permission to
Give them the toodle-oo
Give them the toodle-oo.
Give them the toodle-oo.
Bye-bye.

If you're thinking to yourself, *Wow, that's a bit harsh,* I beg you to reconsider. Couldn't the energy you're spending dealing with a spirit-killing, joy-draining, hope-crushing, icky-pooh person be better spent finding joy in a katrillion other ways? I hope we all know that service is a wonderful way to find joy and happiness in our lives. But *true* service does not involve the manipulative blackmail that negative people try to throw in our faces to keep themselves the center of the universe. Don't fall for it. Your love and friendship are beautiful gifts that, when freely given, can bring some of the greatest and most perfect moments of happiness you'll ever know. But the key to those moments is that they are *your* choice, inspired by the One who knows better than you what's going on at that very moment.

CHAPTER 10

FINDING HAPPINESS IN A GLOBAL ECONOMIC CRISIS

Some folks may postpone going on a Mission 2B☺ because of a global economic crisis. This handbook is going to go out on a limb and suggest that such conditions create the *most* perfect time to go on such a mission. Ironically enough, it's a Mission 2B☺ belief that more people will be showing us how to find happiness during a global economic crisis than at any other time. Why? Because people are going to be compelled to help each other. Start this instant and look around (not on television, but around-around, like in your neighborhood, your city, your state), and you'll be amazed at how good people are. Celebrating the existence of so much goodness adds to your own happiness. It's inspiring. To remind us where to look, I've added this anthem to the Mission 2B☺ mix. As you listen, let your mind lock in the ways you've seen people shine in your life. You'll smile.

See Us Shine

Someone shows some kindness;
Someone gives their time;
Someone helps a neighbor;
See us shine.
Someone lifts a brother
As he falls behind;
Someone shares his burden—
See us shine.

See us shining everywhere:
Every color, every kind.
At the dawning of a brighter day,
Hope will lead the way and see us shine.

Someone says, "I'm sorry";
Someone knows it's time,
Time for some forgiveness:
See us shine.

See us shining everywhere:
Hope is in our hearts and minds.

They're reminding us it's no surprise.
Love is everywhere, just see us shine.

And it doesn't matter where you are,
Some heart will be shining.
There's a method in the gladness
To stop the madness:
See us shine.

Someone throws a line out;
Someone holds and climbs;
Someone's there to catch them;
See us shine.

See them shining everywhere:
Every color, every kind.
At the dawning of a brighter age,
Hope will lead the way
And see us shine, shine, shine, shine,
Hope will lead the way and
See us shine.

This song has plenty of clues to help us find happiness through service, thoughtfulness, friendship, and forgiveness. But the song by itself isn't sufficient to make the point of this chapter of the handbook. The happiness we find in serving and "loving our neighbors as ourselves" begins with our closest neighbors: our families.

Speaking from the perspective of a "provider," I'm acknowledging right here that we sometimes have a tendency to equate the evidence of our love with the amount of material security or possessions we can provide. Hence, when the state of the economy dictates that we can't provide as we once could, we might misunderstand how successful we are at serving our loved ones.

That's why this chapter demands another song, edited onto the end of the "See Us Shine" tune. The handbook presents this song to help providers with little or no dough-re-mi express their love to their families.

What D'ya Got

My girl worries that the end is comin'.
How can we live on next to nothin'?
She's busy stretchin' out every dollar,
So no more gourmet dining or beauty parlors . . .
And I'm tellin' her:

What d'ya got when the well runs dry?
What d'ya got when you can't get by?

What d'ya got when the mortgage rises
Unaccountably?
What d'ya got when the cupboard's bare?
What d'ya got in the Frigidaire?
What d'ya got when there's nothin' there?
Baby, you got me, ain't that enough?
Well, you got me—that ain't so tough.

My kids focus too much on pleasure;
They think Dad's sittin' on a buried treasure.
I got a message that might surprise them
When their old man can't subsidize them.
And I'm tellin' 'em:

What d'ya got when the checks all bounce?
What d'ya got, kid, that really counts?
What d'ya got when the banks announce
You're a liability?
What d'ya got when you're overdrawn?
What d'ya got when your credit's gone?
What d'ya got that keeps hangin' on?
Well, you got me, ain't that enough?
You got me.

Guess I made a promise back when she was twenty-three:
I'd be there to answer every call.
Even though I couldn't see that there'd be times like these,
I have learned what to say, it's been my way to say it all:

What d'ya got when you're overdrawn?
What d'ya got when your credit's gone?
What d'ya got that keeps hangin' on
For eternity?
What d'ya got when it's all a mess?
What d'ya got now that's not worth less?
What d'ya got they can't repossess?
You got me.

What d'ya got when it turns pitch black?
What d'ya got when there's no Prozac?
What d'ya got when you ain't got jack?
Can't you see?
What d'ya got when your dreams get squashed?
What d'ya got when your wires get crossed?
What d'ya got that just won't get lost?
Baby, you got me, ain't that enough?
You got me.

When times are tough economically, we can show the ones we love how much we love them by simply *being there.* It's not the stuff we give them that counts, it's the love. And people on a Mission 2B☺ tell their loved ones how much they love them *a lot!*

It's part of opening ourselves up to the happiness we might be missing.

If you'll remember the previous chapters that talked about being authentic and true to ourselves, keep in mind, that still applies. Your unique way of saying "I love you" still holds. Do it your special way, but make it a habit. Make it sincere, but do it. And when you can't find the "perfect way" to say it or show it, trust the Source of all love to guide you. No sincere effort to express true love is ignored on either side of heaven. That's a Mission 2B☺ axiom.

CHAPTER 11

Unlike Other Missions

Reminder: A Mission 2B☺ is not a proselyting mission. You're not on this mission to convert anyone but yourself to the particulars of learning how to live happily. There's no responsibility to teach investigators how to find the happiness they've been missing, or to testify how you found yours. It's not that you're being selfish by not shouting from the rooftops your discoveries about happiness. But the energy you spend trying to tell others all about finding happiness will be energy un-spent getting better at finding it yourself.

On this Mission 2B☺ you may be tempted to believe that whatever you do to make someone else happy will give you complete fulfillment and make you whole. *Wrong.* If your happiness depends on the happiness of others, then you're doomed to miss the moments. You can't *make* people hear what you want them to hear or do what you want them to do. Grieving over that will prevent you—and them—from finding joy. Joy comes from accepting every soul's God-designed right to learn by his or her own experience; it comes from greater understanding, deeper forgiveness, more sincere listening, exploring, and questioning. Ultimately it comes from trusting that the Source of all happiness is God Himself . . . and trusting that He is capable of giving all the people we love and serve and care about their own perfectly crafted answers to the questions they sincerely ask Him.

So how do we know if we're succeeding? There's only one statistic for how we're doing on this mission: who we are becoming and how much closer we feel to the true Source of happiness.

I know, I know, it's much tougher to measure our success that way than by how much we weigh, or how white our teeth are when we smile in the mirror, or how perfectly our hair cascades over our shoulders. But remember, this is a Mission 2B☺, not a Day Spa 2B☺.

But it's a fact that when Mormons go on a Mission 2B☺, they often can't help wanting to teach the truths they've found to be precious in their lives. It's in the Mormon DNA to be a missionary 24/7. I know how true this is, and that's why I've added this advice in the form of another Mission 2B☺ song.

Use Words

If you wanna spread the good news
To every corner of the world,
If you wanna share the great truths
And let the banner be unfurled,

If you wanna spread the gospel,
Remember, love is a verb.
And only when it's necessary,
Use words.

If you wanna lift a brother,
Reach out your hand.
If you wanna bless a sister,
Listen 'til you understand.
If you wanna teach a lesson
That will truly be heard,
Only when it's necessary, use words.
Only when it's necessary, use words.
Only when it's necessary, use words.

If you let your faith show
By the path you choose to walk,
You'll watch the goodwill grow and grow
More than you will if you just talk and talk
        and talk and talk and talk and talk . . .
If you wanna send a message
To make the world a better place,

It's not a chore, it's a privilege,
Just put a smile on your face.
Let your service be your sermon,
And then maybe afterwards,
Only when it's necessary,
Only when it's necessary,
When it's really necessary,
Use words.

Rap

I know you may find it ironic what I'm choosin' to do
I mean, I'm endin' this exchange by simply talkin' to you
But don't you find the ones that really can influence you best
Are the ones who seem to pass the "what they do is cool" test
They find the simplest ways to make this life a little better
In the spirit of the law and not just the letter
And their actions really make ya wanna follow their lead
With perfect harmony in both word and deed
They're kinda long on action and short on words
They know it's what they do today that's really what gets heard

'Cause aren't ya tired of the ones who only know how to talk
They like to tell the world all about the paths to walk
But when it comes to finding fresh and helpful solutions
To the problems we face, they choose elocution
They can analyze, excessively debating the facts
But don't you love the guy who simply knows how to act
Sometimes there's too little action, but talking is ample
I'll take the individual who leads by example
The way they serve a sister and reach out to a brother
The way they're true and kind to one another

I'll tell you somethin' 'bout me, my friends and peers
I care about what I see more than about what I hear
And even if you think I'm bein' disingenuous
I got a true confession I'd like you to keep between us
I don't care all that much about the way the songs sound
I want the kernel of truth to be the thing that gets found
And if the melody gets hooked into a part of your brain
I hope you're seein' what I'm meanin' in the simple refrain
Wish I could paint it on your spirit so you'd see it each day
Wish I could dance it on your memory to move you some way
Wish I could plant it in your heart so it would grow and grow
Because there's not much I can say to help you come to know

The Importance of the Journal

It is my conviction that this handbook can qualify as a "handbook" (and not a "volume") *only* if it can be digested in one sitting—or maybe walking, jogging, exercising, or whatever you can do while listening to your iPod.

So, this chapter will be the last part assembled by me. After this, you will find pages for your own notes. Mostly these pages are a place where you can chronicle the moments when you find and experience happiness. I believe that this happens most often when unselfish love is given. Some righteously inclined, live-to-serve Christians will interpret this incorrectly, thinking it applies only to when we give love to others. Not so. Jesus told us to love God and others *as ourselves.* There's going to be something phony about our love to others if it doesn't come from a place of gratitude and joy for ourselves—our unique, quirky, interesting selves. All three loves are required: love of God, love of others, and love of self. When we find the moments where all of these "loves" are in perfect balance, we will have perfect moments.

That's why I believe it's important that we keep track of these perfect moments. It's why it's so important to keep a Mission 2B☺ Journal. To *not* write down these moments is like saying we don't appreciate the most precious gifts of life.

As a practical matter, I'm afraid that if I don't write things down, I'll miss the happiness that comes from remembering the unexpected joys that came on the mission. I'm happy to forget the lousy moments, but in my impending senility I don't want to lose the great stuff.

So here's what I'm going to do: I'm going to be keeping my Mission 2B☺ Journal online at http://missiontobehappy.com. What did I find today? What is it that is teaching me to speak the language of joy? What are the things that are adding to, or detracting from, my quest? What will I learn from:

- giving myself a break
- serving those I love
- learning to love someone new to my life
- forgiving
- forgetting
- learning something new
- pampering myself (code for fly fishing)
- discovering a new thought
- easing pain
- accepting life as it is rather than demanding it be the way I want it to be

- accomplishing something
- resting
- healing
- making a plan
- not having any plans
- being surprised
- surprising someone else
- being honest
- following a spiritual impression
- praying

I'll be posting my journal and will also be inviting you to join me at concerts I'll be calling "zone conferences" around the country. I look forward to seeing you and cheering you on in your mission and your quest to be celebrating daily all the ways that we've been blessed. In those moments we'll find . . .

Something Perfect

There's an ache that's missing today.
There's an emptiness that's been filled.
There's a cloud that's lifting and drifting away;
There's a raging storm that's been stilled.

There's a joy that's real,
There's a wound that's finally healed,
There's a future replacing a past.
There's a breath of new life in the cast.

And there's something perfect
Happening here,
And this moment will bury
The mountains of fear,
And through countless tomorrows
It won't disappear,
This something that's perfect
Happening here.

No one knows, so no one can say
That tomorrow all will be well.
Will the brightest promise that shines on today
Shine tomorrow? No one can tell.
But one thing is sure,
And will be forever more:
When such unselfish love has been given,
The world just made more room for heaven.

And there's something perfect
Happening here,
And this moment will bury
The mountains of fear,
And through countless tomorrows
It won't disappear,
This something that's perfect
Happening here.

MISSION TO BE HAPPY
JOURNAL

Unexpected Joys

_____

_____

_____

_____

_____

_____

_____

_____

_____

_____

_____

_____

_____

_____

_____

_____

_____

_____

_____

_____

☺

Surprising Service That Made Me Happier Than I Thought

_____

_____

_____

_____

_____

_____

_____

_____

_____

_____

_____

_____

_____

_____

_____

_____

_____

_____

_____

_____

☺

Personal Pampering That Works

_____

_____

_____

_____

_____

_____

_____

_____

_____

_____

_____

_____

_____

_____

_____

_____

_____

_____

_____

_____

_____

_____

☺

People I'm Giving the Toodle-oo To

☺

Diversities That Make Me Smile

☺

Oooooooooooh Moments

_____

_____

_____

_____

_____

_____

_____

_____

_____

_____

_____

_____

_____

_____

_____

_____

_____

_____

_____

_____

☺

Gifts I've Received That Make Me Smile

_____

_____

_____

_____

_____

_____

_____

_____

_____

_____

_____

_____

_____

_____

_____

_____

_____

_____

_____

_____

_____

_____

☺

Gifts I've Given That Make Me Smile

_____
_____
_____
_____
_____
_____
_____
_____
_____
_____
_____
_____
_____
_____
_____
_____
_____
_____
_____
_____
_____
_____
_____

☺

☺

FREQUENTLY ASKED QUESTIONS

Is a Mission 2B☺ expensive?

Can I afford to do this?

Do I need a companion?

Are there age restrictions?

Is there a military deferment?

Can I have my own songs?

Is there a schedule?

Is this a joke, or is this a real mission?

Who releases me?

Are there prep days?

Can I just quit doing things I already know for sure it's impossible for me to find joy in doing (like the laundry)?

Are there reunions?

Do I get a name tag or a T-shirt?

Who do I call if I want to go home (even though I understand you can't actually go home because you don't really *go* anywhere)?

Do I have to keep track of mileage?

Will somebody feed me or do I have to arrange my own dinner appointments?

Music Credits

All songs written by Michael McLean except:
See Us Shine and What D'ya Got by John Batdorf and Michael McLean
Something Perfect by Tyler Castleton and Michael McLean

Recorded, mixed, and mastered by Guy Randle at Rosewood Recording Co., Provo, UT, except:
See Us Shine and What D'ya Got, recorded and mixed by John Batdorf and David Appelt, BatMac Studio, West Hills, CA

Rhythm tracks created, arranged, and performed by:
Michael Dowdle: Guitars
Brett Raymond: Piano and keyboards
Rob Honey: Bass
Todd Sorenson: Drums and percussion
except: See Us Shine, What D'ya Got, Someone Else, and Something Perfect

Mission To Be Happy
Lead vocal: Michael McLean
Produced by Michael McLean and Guy Randle
© 2007 Shining Star Music (ASCAP)

Sick 'n Tired
Lead vocal: Michael McLean
Background vocals: John Batdorf
Produced by Michael McLean, Staci Peters, and Guy Randle
© 2007 Shining Star Music (ASCAP)

Pills
Lead vocal: Michael McLean
Background vocals: John Batdorf
Produced by Michael McLean and Guy Randle
© 2009 Shining Star Music (ASCAP)

MUSIC CREDITS

YOU DON'T KNOW
Vocals: Rick Logan
Produced by Michael McLean and Guy Randle
© 2007 Shining Star Music (ASCAP)

WITH PAUL AND JOHN
Lead vocal: Michael McLean
Background vocals: John Batdorf
Produced by Michael McLean and Guy Randle
© 2009 Shining Star Music (ASCAP)

I DON'T NEED A SIGN
Vocals: John Batdorf
Produced by Michael McLean and Guy Randle
© 2009 Shining Star Music (ASCAP)

**SOMEONE ELSE/FIND OUT WHO I AM/
   YOU'RE NOT THE SEQUEL**
Lead vocals: Katie Thompson and Randy Porter
Produced by Michael McLean and Guy Randle
© 2009 Shining Star Music (ASCAP)

ONE
Lead vocals: April Meservy and Chad Neth
Produced by Staci Peters, Guy Randle and
   Michael McLean
© 2007 Shining Star Music (ASCAP)

THE TOODLE-OO
Lead vocal: Michael McLean
Background vocals: John Batdorf

Produced by Michael McLean and Guy Randle
© 2009 Shining Star Music (ASCAP)

SEE US SHINE
Vocals: John Batdorf
Produced and arranged by John Batdorf
© 1992 Shining Star Music (ASCAP)

WHAT D'YA GOT
Vocals: John Batdorf
Produced and arranged by John Batdorf
© 2008 Batmac Music (BMI)/Shining Star Music
   (ASCAP)

USE WORDS
Lead vocal: Katie Thompson
Rap vocal: Michael McLean
Background vocals: Kristen Randle, Tanya
   Barkdull, and Jessie Funk
Produced by Michael McLean and Guy Randle
Arranged by Todd Sorensen
© 2005 Shining Star Music (ASCAP)

SOMETHING PERFECT
Lead vocal: Chad Neth
Background vocal: April Meservy
Produced by Tyler Castleton and Michael
   McLean
Arranged by Tyler Castleton
© 2007 Shining Star Music (ASCAP)/Diamond
   Aire Music (ASCAP)